REAL

mvpkids®

The Way We're Made

Sophia Day®

Written by Megan Johnson   Illustrated by Stephanie Strouse

The Sophia Day® Creative Team-
Megan Johnson, Stephanie Strouse, Marla Conn,
Kayla Pearson, Timothy Zowada, Carol Sauder, Mel Sauder

A **special thank you** to our team of reviewers who graciously
give us feedback, edits and help ensure that our products
remain accurate, applicable and genuinely diverse.

Published and Distributed by MVP Kids Media, LLC -
Mesa, Arizona, USA
Printed by RR Donnelley Asia Printing Solutions, Ltd -
Dongguan City, Guangdong Province, China

Designed by Stephanie Strouse

ISBN 978-164370762-4
DOM May 2019,
Job # 11-003-01

May your childhood be filled with adventure, your days with hope and your learnings with wisdom, and may you continuously grow as an MVP Kid, preparing to lead a responsible, meaningful life.

- SOPHIA DAY

Search the land
and sail the seas!
You'll find there's no one
just like me.

There's not a thing
that I would trade.
I like myself
the way I'm made!

What do you like about yourself?

In all the world

you will not find

a fingerprint

that's just like mine.

Nor a soul

or heart the same.

I am good

the way I'm made.

Sparkling eyes

    of blue or brown,

green or hazel,

    narrow, round.

Eyes of any

    shape or shade,

I am good

    the way I'm made.

Hair that's brown,
 red or blonde,
black or white,
 short or long.
Straight or curly,
 waves or braids,
I am good
 the way I'm made.

What color hair
do you have?

Birthmarks, freckles,
dark and light.
Countless colors-
a beautiful sight!
Skin comes in many
different shades.
I am good
the way I'm made.

Some kids are big

some are small,

round or thin,

short or tall.

Any kind of

size or shape,

I am good

the way I'm made.

Sometimes kids

    use hands to talk,

touch to see

    or wheels to walk.

We'll find creative

    ways to play.

I am good

    the way I'm made.

How do you
like to play?

Don't look just
at what you see.
There's more inside
that makes me *me.*

Heart of kindness,
hands that help,
putting friends
before myself.
I discovered
while we played,
you are good
the way you're made.

How are you
a good friend?

Art and books,

sports and balls,

building rockets,

loving dolls.

Each of us

have different strengths.

We are good

the way we're made.

What are you
good at?

It isn't hard

for us to see

I'm not like you;

You're not like me.

We can do things

different ways

and celebrate

the way we're made!

Why do we celebrate differences?

meet our

mvpkids®

featured in
The Way We're Made™

Yong Chen

Sarah Goldstein

Gabby Gonzalez

Annie James

Blake James

Liam Johnson

Ezekiel Jordan

Faith Jordan

LeBon Miller

Lucas Miller

Miriam Nasser

Aanya Patel

Julia Rojas

Frankie Russo

Leo Russo

Olivia Wagner

HELPFUL TEACHING TIPS
Head. Heart. Hand.

Informing Minds

A strong self-esteem sets children up for success in all areas. Children with a strong self-esteem have the confidence to take risks, develop skills and feel prepared for everyday challenges. In contrast, kids with a low self-esteem have trouble making decisions, trying new challenges and building friendships.

The term "self-talk" refers to a way a child thinks and talks about himself or herself. A child's self-talk is directly linked to self-esteem and success.

Several researchers suggest that there should ideally be a 5:1 ratio of positive interactions for every negative interaction a child experiences. Keep this in mind when correcting and interacting with your child.

Moving Hearts

The way parents speak to their children often becomes the child's inner voice. Take time to evaluate your language, the tone of your voice and the way you want your children to think about themselves.

In the preschool years, most of a child's experiences and vocabulary are driven by parents, caregivers and media. It is critical for parents to model healthy self-talk. If your child is using negative self-talk, examine your own thoughts about yourself and refrain from using negative words to describe yourself.

Body image is a significant factor in self-esteem. Body image is shaped by the cultural messages our children receive every day. It is never too early to discuss with children the way that media influences how they see themselves.

The most significant factors in low self-esteem often stem from an authority figure who is disapproving, absent or preoccupied, or when authority figures are in conflict with one another. Examine the influences in your child's life and try to eliminate undue criticism and distractions and reduce conflict in your child's environment.

Children can be taught cultural sensitivity and awareness. Dismantle stereotypes by exposing your child to a variety of media that shows people of different ethnicity, body shapes and sizes in a positive light.

To be most effective, encouragement and affirmation need to be true, specific and focused on the qualities you want to encourage. For example, "You worked very hard" is more motivating than "you are so smart", and "you did a great job brushing your hair all by yourself" is more beneficial than "you are so pretty."

Help your child keep a journal. Even as a preschooler your child can circle an expression to show how he feels that day and have a parent help with the writing. Journaling shows your child that his thoughts, feelings and experiences matter.

Be direct and factual about differences. Use simple but correct terms to describe your child's (or their playmate's) health conditions, behavioral needs or appearance. This will show your child that their differences are okay to talk about and not something of which you or they are ashamed:

Judgment	Observation
"What's wrong with...?"	"What's different about...?"
(not) normal	(not) typical
weird, freaky, ugly	unusual, unique, different
retarded, crazy, stupid	thinks differently, brain works differently
fat, thin, short, other body description	built differently

Common	Preferred
is special needs/ special needs child	has special needs/ child with special needs
is autistic/ autistic child* (*Down Syndrome, etc.*)	has autism/ a child with autism* (*Down Syndrome, etc.*)
is adopted	was adopted
real family/parent	birth family/ parent (*step and adoptive parents and families are real*)

some parents don't mind, or even prefer, to describe their child with his or her diagnosis first as a way to celebrate how that diagnosis makes their child special. When you get to know someone, you can ask which they prefer.

Directing
Hands

For additional
tip and reference
information, visit
www.mvpkids.com.

Grow up with our mvpkids®

Celebrate!™ Paperbacks

Ages 4-8

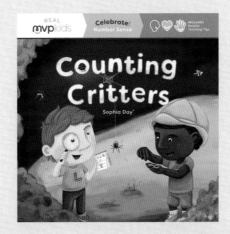

Celebrate! Number Sense
REAL mvpkids
Counting Critters
Sophia Day®

Celebrate! Self-Esteem
REAL mvpkids
The Way We're Made
Sophia Day®

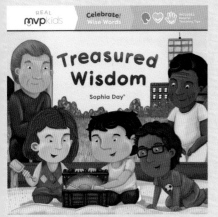

Celebrate! Wise Words
REAL mvpkids
Treasured Wisdom
Sophia Day®

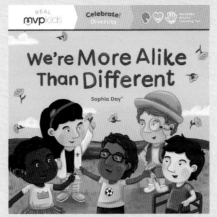

Celebrate! Diversity
REAL mvpkids
We're More Alike Than Different
Sophia Day®

Our **Celebrate!™** paperback books for Pre-K to Grade 2 focus on social, emotional, educational and physical needs. Helpful Teaching Tips are included in each book to equip mentors and parents. Also available are expertly written curriculum and interactive e-book apps. These books are perfect for classrooms and home schooling!

Inspire Me-Books™

- *Inspire Character®, Enrich Entertainment™, Nurture Literacy™, Expand Education™ and Cultivate Mentorship™ with our interactive* **InspireMe-book™** *apps. These apps are designed to expand the experience of our content.*
- *Functions include audio of Sophia Day reading the book, learn-to-read options such as slow reading with highlighted words or choosing a specific word to be pronounced along with interactive games.*

www.mvpkids.com

Yong Chen

Leo Russo

Frankie Russo

Julia Rojas

Aanya Patel

Faith James

Blake James

Sarah Goldstein